OLD COTTAGES,
FARM HOUSES, AND
OTHER HALF-TIMBER BUILDINGS IN SHROPSHIRE, HEREFORDSHIRE, AND CHESHIRE

THE OLD RECTORY, EARDISLAND.

Frontispiece.

OLD COTTAGES, FARM HOUSES, AND
OTHER HALF-TIMBER BUILDINGS

IN SHROPSHIRE, HEREFORDSHIRE,
AND CHESHIRE

ILLUSTRATED ON ONE HUNDRED PLATES

REPRODUCED IN COLLOTYPE FROM

A SPECIAL SERIES OF PHOTOGRAPHS

TAKEN BY

JAMES PARKINSON
Architectural Woodworker.

WITH INTRODUCTORY AND DESCRIPTIVE NOTES
AND NUMEROUS SKETCHES

By E. A. OULD, F.R.I.B.A.

CLASSIC EDITIONS

This edition digitally re-mastered and
published by JM Classic Editions © 2007
Original text and images © EA Ould & J Parkinson 1904

ISBN 978-1-905217-71-7

All rights reserved. No part of this book subject
to copyright may be reproduced in any form or
by any means without prior permission in writing
from the publisher.

PREFACE.

WHEN an author sits down to write a book he is usually justified in assuming that such of the public as may go the length of purchasing his work will proceed to read it. But in the present instance the writer is oppressed by an uneasy suspicion that the attractions of Mr. Parkinson's seductive photographs will prove sufficient for the majority of readers, who will be content to let the venerable subjects here represented tell their own tale in their own way, and will consider the presence of a showman almost an impertinence.

It may, nevertheless, be of interest to the more serious student to consider a little more closely the characteristics of the timber architecture of these Western Counties, and to compare them with those of black-and-white buildings in other parts of the country; while even the unthinking amateur may find his imagination quickened and his interest heightened by hearing something about the construction of these examples, the materials employed, and the colouring produced, from one who has studied nearly every subject upon the spot. So I will take heart and proceed to address my small but select audience, and to invite them to follow me from Shrewsbury southwards, through Much Wenlock and Ludlow to Stokesay, and from thence through the beautiful by-ways of Herefordshire, until they terminate at Ledbury on the borders of Worcestershire, and afterwards to turn back and explore the broad plains of Cheshire, where black-and-white houses of all sorts and sizes are as common as the magpies which they so much resemble.

E. A. OULD.

LIVERPOOL, *May*, 1904.

LIST OF PLATES

ARRANGED ALPHABETICALLY UNDER TOWNS AND
VILLAGES IN EACH COUNTY.

SHROPSHIRE.

	Plate
BEWDLEY, Cottage at	11
BRIDGENORTH, Bishop Percy's House	9
BROMFIELD, Cottages at	19
,, The Priory Gate-house	20
CLEVEDON, Cottage at	10
CRAVEN ARMS, House at	14
,, ,, (back of)	15
,, A demolished House from	16
CRESSAGE, House at	18
DODMORE FARM, near Ludlow	21, 22
LUDFORD HOUSE	27
,, ,, Bay of	28
,, The Bell Inn	26
LUDLOW, House in Street	24
,, Lane's Asylum	23
,, The Reader's House	25
,, See DODMORE FARM.	
MUCH WENLOCK, House at	5
,, Houses and Shops	6

LIST OF PLATES.

	Plate
MUCH WENLOCK, A Corner House	7
„ The Abbot's House	8
PITCHFORD HALL, A Gable-End from	17
RICHARD'S CASTLE, Farm-house at	29
SHREWSBURY, House in Butcher Row	2
„ House in High Street	3
„ Shops in Butcher Row	1
„ The Court House	4
STOKESAY CASTLE, The Gate-house	13
WORFIELD, Cottages at	12

HEREFORDSHIRE.

	Plate
"Buttas" Falconry, See WEOBLY.	
CHOLSTREY, Farm-house at	39
EARDISLAND, The Old Rectory	40
EARDISLEY, Cottages at	54
„ House at	55
FENHAMPTON, near WEOBLY, Farm-house at	68
HEREFORD, Hall of the Butchers' Guild	69
LEOMINSTER, "The Grange"	38
LUNTLEY, near PEMBRIDGE, Farm-house at	52
„ The Dovecote	53
LEDBURY, Clerks' Houses	70
„ Houses in Church Row	71
„ The Market Hall	72
LITTLE HEREFORD, Cottages at	73
MIDDLEBROOK FARM, near PEMBRIDGE	47
„ Farm Buildings at	48
„ Cottages at	49

LIST OF PLATES. ix

		Plate
ORLETON COURT		30
,,	Cottage in a Lane	34
,,	Farm Buildings at	36
,,	House in Main Street	33
,,	Old House at	31
,,	Roadside House near	35
,,	The Church Porch	37
,,	"The Seven Gables"	32
PEMBRIDGE, Cottages at		43, 50, 51
,,	Farm-house at	44, 45, 46
,,	Houses at Entrance to Village	42, 43
,,	The Village Street	41
,,	See LUNTLEY.	
,,	See MIDDLEBROOK.	
WEOBLY, Cottages at		56, 57
,,	Houses called "The Rows"	61
,,	Houses in Street	62, 63
,,	Old School House	64
,,	,, ,, The Porch	65
,,	"The Buttas" Falconry	66
,,	"The Leys" Farm	58, 59
,,	,, ,, Doorway	60
,,	See FENHAMPTON.	
WIGMORE, View in the Village		67

CHESHIRE.

ALDERLEY EDGE, Cottages at		81, 82
,,	,, Farm-house at	83
,,	,, The Eagle and Child Inn	80

LIST OF PLATES.

	Plate
ALSAGER, See HASLINGTON HALL.	
ADLINGTON, Porch of the Hall	92
BRAMHALL, Parts of the Hall	93, 94
CHESTER, House in Whitefriars	74
,, The Stanley Palace	75
DUDDON HALL, A Gable	76
DUTTON HALL, The Porch	95
GAWSWORTH HALL	90
HANDFORTH HALL	78
HASLINGTON HALL, near ALSAGER	99
LOWER CARDEN HALL	77
MIDDLEWICH OLD HALL	96, 97
MARTON, The Church	87
,, The Hall	88
,, ,, BACK VIEW	89
MORETON OLD HALL, The Gate-house	100
PRESTBURY, The Priest's House	86
SANDBACH, The Boar Inn	98
STANLEY HALL	79
SWINYARD OLD HALL	85
WELTROUGH HALL	91
WOODFORD, The Old Hall	84

LIST OF ILLUSTRATIONS IN THE TEXT.

	Page
Houses in Butchers' Row, Shrewsbury	4
Plan of Bay Window at Ludford House	13
Door of the Hall of the Butchers' Guild, Hereford	16
Oriel Window at the Hall of the Butchers' Guild	17
A Column from the Market Hall, Ledbury	18
Bracket from Cholstrey	19
Detail of Beam from Pembridge	19
Doorway at Middlebrook, with details	20
A Beam from Middlebrook	21
Bargeboards from Middlebrook	21
An Oriel Window at Eardisley	22
Plan and Section of the Oriel shown on previous fig.	23
A Bargeboard near Eardisley	24
Windows from Church Street, Ledbury	27
Plaster Gable at Whitefriars, Chester	28
Detail of Porch at Handforth Hall	30
Embossed Lead Spout from Eagle and Child, Alderley Edge	31
Section of the Lead Spout shewn in previous fig.	31
A Cottage at Alderley Edge	32
Detail of Beam from Stanley Hall, Cheshire	33
Plan of Bays at the Priest's House, Prestbury	34
Lead Glazing at the Priest's House, Prestbury	34
Door at Marton Church with detail	35
Doorway from Marton Hall	36

NOTE.

PLATE 40 is selected for the Frontispiece, and is bound in the front of the book, but is referred to in the text and List of Illustrations under its proper number.

PLATE 3 (title of): *for* "in the High Street, Shrewsbury," *read* "in Frankwell, Shrewsbury."

PLATE 4 (title of): *for* "The Court House, Shrewsbury," *read* "Gate of the Council House, Shrewsbury."

INTRODUCTION.

IN studying the Timber Architecture of these three counties, the most ordinary observer cannot fail to be struck by the difference in general effect, which is apparent between it and the treatment of similar materials, in the Southern and Western Counties, and a comparison of our examples with those in Messrs. Galsworthy Davie and Guy Dawber's charming book,* will illustrate and display these distinctions convincingly. These may be partly due to differences of climate and surroundings, the sunshine of the South and the rainfall of the West laying on their colours and textures very differently in the way of weathering and vegetation, but the habit and fashion of the architecture and construction contribute still more to the widely different result. But when this has been granted and we begin to generalize, we are met by all sorts of difficulties and paradoxes, one of which is, that we occasionally meet with an example in the Western Counties which might have been transported bodily from Kent or Sussex, while a few of the better manor houses in those counties exhibit features and ornament which we assume to belong exclusively to the West. This may of course be the result of accident or may have arisen from an interchange of architects, but in the following remarks we must be understood to

* Old Cottages and Farmhouses in Kent and Sussex, by W. Galsworthy Davie and E. Guy Dawber. Batsford, 1900.

be enunciating only very broad rules and general principles. In the West we think it will be found that the timbers are larger and more massive and the overhangs consequently bolder, while the detail of the moulded parts is less elaborate and coarser, and the carving *as a rule* more primitive. The lavish and sometimes wasteful use of timber is accounted for by the existence of the large forests which are known to have flourished in these three counties, at a safe distance from the iron-smelting works which depleted the woodlands of Sussex, and the ship-building yards of the South, which took the best of the timber available, when "Hearts of oak were our ships." The remoteness of these districts and the absence of roads, navigable rivers and other means of communication with the outer world, while conserving their supply of timber deprived them of the assistance of foreign carvers and craftsmen and of designers from a distance, whose work is discernible in the early buildings of the home counties. Again, the sculpture and carving on the timber buildings we are considering, although more plentiful and elaborate, were not usually the work of trained artists, but the simple, traditional, but, (very often), most effective ornament of the village carpenter. There are marked exceptions to this rule, for the carving on the beams of Stokesay Gate House, (Plate xiii), and the Reader's House at Ludlow, (Plate xxv), will compare favourably with anything of the kind remaining in England. But by far the most marked characteristic of Western design, is the elaboration of ornamental forms in the timber work itself, and this is more apparent the further north you travel, and culminates in the multitudinous forms and ingenious devices appearing in the framing of the Manor Houses of Cheshire and Lancashire—regions which were the last to emerge from the semibarism of the Middle Ages, (Plates lxxviii, lxxxv, and xcix). These designs and patterns were contrived by using the bent and twisted pieces of wood, obtained from the smaller branches, and disposing of them in the panels formed by the uprights and cross rails, so as to present a regular and repetitionary pattern, whether circular, quatrefoil, or lozenge. Plates lxxviii and lxxxiii gives examples of all varieties. This method of decoration is sometimes met with in the South-Eastern counties, as at Mayfield and Great Tangley Manor and elsewhere, but it is quite the exception, and it is difficult to say why it was so very generally adopted in the West. It may have been the natural love of ornament and want of restraint in a less civilised people, but against this may be urged the fact that the later the date of the building the more elaborate the design appears to be : or possibly the builders thought that this constant strutting made the building more rigid and better able to resist the more frequent gales in the West ; but more probably it was suggested by the trees themselves, which, bent and distorted by the force of this constant wind, supplied many more crooked than straight timbers.

It has been computed that the greater part of the timber cottages in England were built between A.D. 1558 and A.D. 1625, the last fifty years of this period being far the most productive, but in the districts under review many houses remain which date from the fifteenth century, such as Butcher Row at Shrewsbury, and the houses called "The Rows," at Weobly, (Plates i and lxi), while the use of timber in the construction of cottages and farm buildings extended well into the eighteenth century in the West, where the Dutch forms and methods of "Queen Anne" architecture were slow to establish themselves.

The fact that so few cottages remain of the fourteenth and fifteenth centuries and the first half of the sixteenth, is partly to be accounted for by the natural decay which has gradually swept them away, and partly that the shocking mortality of the Black Death rendered the building of new cottages unnecessary for many years afterwards : also previous to the Reformation most of the labourers on the land were accommodated in conventual buildings and outhouses, or beneath the roofs of the great lord or land-owner, while the numerous hospitals, bede or alms-houses afforded shelter to a large number more. But when the change of ownership came at the Reformation, an immense impetus was given to agriculture, and the building of cottages became a necessity, as the former shelters and asylums had disappeared.

The system of building with timber has often been described, and it does not appear to have differed greatly in different counties. Stout oak sills are laid horizontally upon a low wall of stone or brick and into these are tenoned upright posts, the larger ones being placed at the external angles. Upon these upright posts, horizontal heads are placed just below the level of the chamber floor, and the intervening spaces formed into panels with thinner pieces, the whole being framed and tenoned together and pinned with oak pins. The joists of the floor are then laid, resting upon the horizontal heads and frequently being

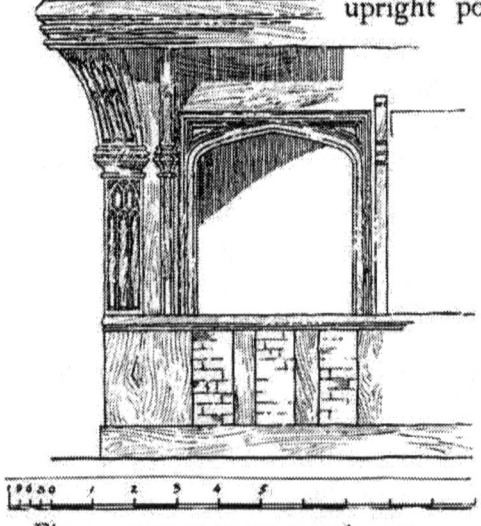

Fig. 1. HOUSES IN BUTCHER'S ROW, SHREWSBURY.

partly supported by internal beams which appear in the ceilings of the house. Upon the ends of the joists, the sill of the upper storey is laid and the framing is more or less a repetition of that below, the head forming a support for the spars of the roof and being frequently carried over at the ends as a wall plate to carry the overhanging gables, Plate xxxv. Where the upper storey overhangs the lower one it is supported on the joist ends, (as shewn in Plate lvi); these are then made stouter for the purpose, and brought over, the ends being frequently rounded or shaped, as at Orleton, Plate xxxiii. Where the upper storey overhangs at the ends as well as in front, the usual expedient is to place strong beams diagonally from the corners to an internal wall (usually appearing in the ceiling) and to tenon the floor joists into it and let them run from it two ways at right angles to the walls of the house. These are called "dragon beams," probably a corruption of "diagonal," (*see* Plate xxxviii). In the older examples the angle post is brought out in the form of a rude corbel to assist in supporting the diagonal beam and superstructure, and these are sometimes carved or panelled, (*see* Plate i). When the framework or skeleton of the building is erected, the spaces or panels between the timbers are filled with lattice work of hazel sticks or laths, intertwined and plastered over flush with the timbers, with clay or loam. Sometimes, where the overhang is not great, bricks were used for the filling in, exposed and sometimes arranged in a herring-bone pattern. The roof timbers were generally framed into the stouter oak uprights, and in the older or more important building these were wrought, shaped, moulded and exposed. The windows were formed in the uprights and cross-timbers which were moulded for the purpose, and were sometimes carried up into the roof to form dormers, but this is not usual in any of the earlier examples, *see* Plates xxxv and lxxxii. The roofs were generally covered in the Western counties with thatch, or with flag-slates, much heavier than the thin Horsham stone slates of Kent and Sussex. A good many of them are now covered with tiles, but this is probably not the original covering, as tiles were little used in England until the seventeenth century, owing to the scarcity of coal and the difficulty of burning them. For the same reason bricks were not employed extensively in England for building before Henry VIII's reign, except in districts where no stone could be procured.

The chimneys are generally of stone, and they are less elaborate and architectural than those in the South. The shafts have often been rebuilt in brick, and those appearing on the ridge of the building are generally of that material. The massive external chimneys are nearly always connected with baking ovens with picturesque flag or tile roofs, and together they form valuable features in the general outline.

DESCRIPTIVE NOTES ON THE PLATES.

THE importance of Shrewsbury historically and politically, and as occupying a prominent position upon both the Severn and the great North Road from London, would prepare us for the number and richness of its buildings and for the refinement displayed in their details. The corner house in Butcher Row, Plate i and Figure 1, is one of the earliest timber buildings in the country, being purely Gothic in character. It probably dates from the early part of the fifteenth century, and is a most interesting example of the open shopfront of mediæval times, of which there are many specimens remaining on the Continent. The carved and richly panelled angle posts on both floors have carried their burden bravely these 500 years, and neither they nor the woodwork generally shew any sign of decay.

The little building further down the same street, Plate ii, is also a marvel constructionally, the two slender brackets supporting the weight of two full storeys, and demonstrating once more what oak is capable of when applied scientifically.

Plate iii shews a building in the High Street which has some purely Salopian features. To divide the plaster panels with balusters instead of with upright timbers is a common device in Shrewsbury, but a very rare one outside it. It may often be noticed that an old town acquires a trick or habit of this sort, which it loves to repeat with many variations. First discovered accidentally by the filling up of some balcony or balustrade, the builder has been struck by the excellence of the effect produced, and has repeated it elsewhere. Nuremberg, Rothenburg, Dordrecht and Lisieux have all little fashions of their own.

The Court House, (Plate iv), has similar balusters to the foregoing, under the upper window, and the pediment over the lower windows, together with the carving and mouldings, herald the approach of the Renaissance. The gradual but complete change which took place in Queen Elizabeth's reign in the detail and design of timber buildings, without departing from the mediæval methods of construction, can further be traced in the Ley's Farm and the Stanley Palace, Chester, (Plates lvii, lviii and lxxvi). Notwithstanding its new fashioned classic dress, this Shrewsbury courtyard and massive gateway are reminiscent of the gate-houses and fortified enclosures of not yet forgotten mediæval times.

Much Wenlock nestles in a valley among the hills of which the Wrekin is the best known. The Roman town of Uriconium is not far off, and the ancient name of the mountain is the root from which both the Roman colony and the Saxon town of Wrekinchester or Wroxeter took their names. A religious house was built at Wenlock in early times, and after the destructive incursion of the Danes, it was rebuilt by Lady Godiva and her Earl Leofric, when Edward the Confessor was king. The Norman builders continued the good work, and for 400 years it was the richest and most important abbey in Shropshire.

The Abbot's House (Plate viii) is one of the most perfect examples of its kind, and it is still tenanted and beautifully kept up. The picturesque bell-turret is of timber framing, which is our only excuse for giving this seductive view to our readers. Dominated by the ruined abbey, the little town seems to seek its protection in charming dependence, and numerous timber buildings abound. The three we have selected are typical examples.

The first, Plate v, is built upon the ruins of the old conventual buildings, probably the tithe-barn. The timber structure is delightfully promiscuous and unsymmetrical, but wholly satisfactory. The timbering of the gable is quite unique in arrangement but strictly constructional. Partly flagged and partly tiled, as a piece of colour it is wonderful, especially when the autumn tints have fired the Virginia creeper.

The next, (Plate vi), shews a house in a main street which might well serve as a model for modern street architecture, as it furnishes excellent shop fronts, and a covered porch on the ground floor, and cosy deep-recessed bay windows and a balcony on the first floor, where the front wall is set back. With flower boxes on the balcony, what a rich note of colour might be given to the street. The non-constructional ornamentation of the bay fronts marks a late period and the first sign of decadence.

Very different in the latter respect is the third example, (Plate vii), the very perfection of simplicity. The builder of this little corner house put in windows where he wanted light, and timber struts where they could best do their work, and he left its fate to Providence and its decoration to Time (the one to preserve it, and the other to adorn it), and the result to-day only shews us how well both have served him.

As a contrast, the house at Bridgenorth of Bishop Percy, the writer of the *Reliques*, is valuable, (Plate ix). Tradition says that he was born here, but it seems more likely that he built it in his later prosperous days, when he, the son of a Bridgenorth grocer, changed his father's name of Piercy for the more aristocratic Percy. Although somewhat showy and overdone, it is a fine example, and carries its years lightly; but if all three dormers had followed the design of the one to the right, the effect would have been more peaceful and less frivolous, as becomes the house of a bishop.

In marked contrast once more are Plates x, xi and xii, simple Shropshire cottages, never, most likely, having known the blessings of a father, in the shape of an architect; but having been born of that great Mother, necessity, and clothed with whatever materials were most handy, they were left to shift for themselves. Scarcely worth perpetuating, you will say; but as studies of buildings suiting to perfection their site and surroundings, they are worth, we think, more than passing notice.

Plate xiii shews perhaps the most beautiful gatehouse in the world—none the less beautiful for having been drawn and photographed oftener than any professional beauty; but any notice of timber architecture in Shropshire would be incomplete without at least one view of this pathetic monument. Mr. Parkinson seems to have quite caught the spirit of the original, and has given enough of the surroundings to shew how perfectly it suits them. Originally the castle of the great family of the Says, the Norman lords of Stoke, Stokesay stands, with its gatehouse, its grey towers and its parish church, as complete, deserted and solitary, as the group of hoary buildings known as Pisa, which once seen can never be forgotten.

The house at Craven Arms, illustrated on Plates xiv and xv, produced an impression upon us which the photographs seem hardly to justify, but grouping and perfect colouring are, after all, as important as richness of detail, and if your imagination can replace the good old windows, you will, as it were, restore eyeballs to the sightless face.

The second house at Craven Arms, Plate xvi, has alas disappeared, but by the courtesy of Mr. Harper, the local photographer, we are allowed to reproduce this picture, which he took before its demolition. It was a very beautiful example, and its disappearance is a sad loss to the neighbourhood.

A study of Pitchford Hall seems to shew that the timber style is not the best for a large mansion. The little corner of it shown on

Plate xvii, is charming, but when you see three sides of a huge quadrangle all in black and white and all in one style, without any curved pieces or variety of any sort, the effect is wearisome in the extreme, and irresistibly suggests the zebra !

Plate xviii, *Cressage*. The name is a contraction of Christ's oak, but the legend relating to the tree does not appear to have survived. The house is a very fine example, and has been well kept up. The quaint oriel window is of course a later addition, and at night when illuminated, it must have the appearance of a lantern hanging upon the gable. The sturdy balusters of the porch have been filled with modern sashes, as people became less tolerant of draughts. The fine mass of diagonal chimney shafts assists the grouping amazingly.

Timber framing never seems so happy as when it has a cap of thatch, which indulgently accommodates itself to its irregular lines and vagaries. Plate xix is an excellent example of this, and the grand outside chimney and oven of masonry rear themselves until they are lost indefinably in the brickwork of the chimney shaft. To appreciate the perfection of this example one must have tried this blending of stone and brickwork in modern walling.

The remains of the Gothic gateway of Bromfield Priory, Plate xx, were requisitioned in Jacobean times to do service as the base for a timber superstructure, and yet no incongruity appears in the composition.

Plates xxi and xxii illustrate Dodmore Hall, one of the most perfect untouched examples in England. It will be found by the diligent seeker on the side of a hill near Ludlow, in the midst of fields far away from any road, surrounded by a high and singularly beautiful brick wall. Behind this it successfully resisted for long enough the attempts to photograph it, until a point of view was at length discovered after a third visit. The verge boards and pendants are original and very delicate, and the timbers have never been blackened, but have a texture like velvet. Both the first and second floors overhang considerably, the upper ones being entirely carried upon the beam and joist ends, and it will be noticed that the timbering is lighter in the gables, so as to diminish the load. The bay makes no pretence of being self-supporting, but has two crutches, while some buttresses lend their assistance to the overhanging first floor on one side.

Lane's Hospital at Ludlow, Plate xxiii, is not a good group, but it is genuine, while the detail is most interesting and the carving most effective.

Another example in the same town, (Plate xxiv), is probably by the same builder and of the same age. Traces of the projecting windows remain, and these must be restored in imagination before the true effect of this well-balanced little street front can be estimated.

The Reader's House at Ludlow, (Plate xxv), is too well known to require any description. It has been so surrounded by the temporary sheds in the churchyard, that no point of view can be found to do justice to its refined carving and matchless proportions.

Plate xxvi shews what remains of the old Bell coaching inn at Ludford. It has been restored with much energy but with little knowledge, and the photograph is only admitted on account of the timbering of the main gable, which, even without its projecting windows, is very beautiful.

Ludford House, Plates xxvii and xxviii, is an interesting and highly architectural composition in masonry and timber work, and the modern slated roof, although most unfortunate, cannot deprive it of its picturesque quality. One cannot help suspecting that the massive grey rubble walls below formed part of some earlier building. The method by which this wall is reduced in thickness by a slated weathering, to take the thinner-timbered wall above, should be noted: also the curious plan of the grand stone bay, with its square unmoulded head, (Figure 2). This house is hidden behind the old church, and together they form a little peaceful courtyard which is very attractive and "old world."

Plate xxix. Farm-house. Richard's Castle. Of the castle, which was one of the earliest in the kingdom, dating from before the Norman Conquest, little remains but heaps of grass-grown masonry. The farm house is a good example of plain timbering, just saved from monotony by the weather-boarding and the delicate ornament in the gable.

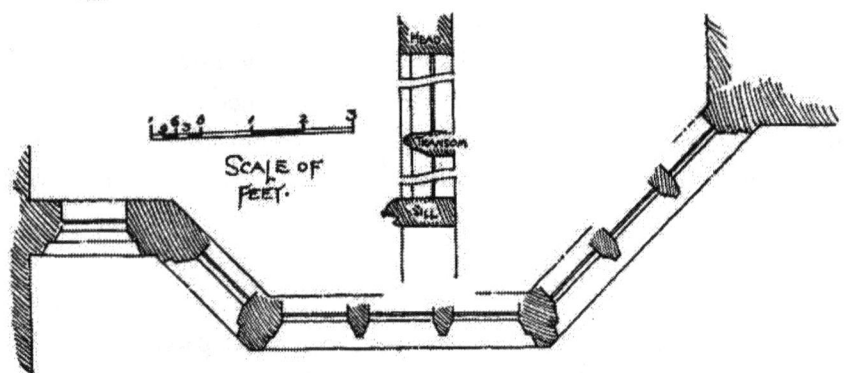

Fig. 2. PLAN OF THE BAY WINDOW AT LUDFORD HOUSE.

Crossing the boundary into HEREFORDSHIRE, the first village of interest is Orleton, which abounds in timber buildings of high merit. Orleton Court, (Plate xxx), has been restored but it retains many original features. It was the residence of the Blount family and Pope stayed here when paying his addresses to Miss Blount. The room over the porch is known as his study.

The subject of Plate xxxi is more satisfactory, although shorn of its beautiful projecting windows and oriels, the seats of which still remain. The hoary grey timbers, the pink stone base, the bold overhang and shapely brackets, and the pathetic little garden seat, enable one to picture what this charming little house must have been in its prime.

The next view, Plate xxxii, shews the back of a large Farm House at Orleton, called "The Seven Gables," and from all sides it is quite satisfactory. The roofs, partly of flags and partly tiles, seem aglow with crimson, purple and emerald. What breadth and generosity appear in the fine dormers (not all window, like modern ones) and the ample chimney breast, with the shaft turned anglewise to comfortably stop the overhanging eaves.

Plate xxxiii shews another house in the main street, which it would be difficult to improve upon, unless one could call back the oriel window in the gable, where the solid moulded sill remains. The characteristic colouring of the district again appears in the mingled stone and brick and flag slates. The sides of the joists supporting the overhanging gable have been painted white with good effect.

Plate xxxiv is a cottage in a quiet lane, possessed of qualities to which no photograph can do justice, and which no words can describe. The flagged roof of the shed in front has been patched with red tiles by some inspired but unconscious genius, and the plaster panels of the timbering coloured an orange buff.

Again the beautiful oriel has been snatched from the gable of Plate xxxv, leaving the sill and pretty bracket, both sufficiently massive and constructional to resist removal. The combined chimney and high dormer form a curious piece of grouping.

Plate xxxvi shews what farm buildings might be, and in the background, what, alas, many modern ones are!

Plate xxxvii has no business in a work solely devoted to domestic architecture, but it pleaded so hard for admission, assuring us that there was nothing distinctively "churchy" about it, that we had not the heart to refuse!

IN HEREFORDSHIRE.

We are now in the heart of Herefordshire, that county of purple soil, wooded hills, and blue distances; where friendly white-faced cattle look a shy welcome over luxuriant hedge-tops, and masses of white violets nestle beneath; where the apple-blossom clothes the Spring in pink and white, and the mistletoe embraces apple-tree and oak with indiscriminate affection.

Leominster is the first town we come to of any size. The fine church is all that remains of the abbey founded by Leofric, the lord of Lady Godiva. The ducking stool is preserved in the church, to the great indignation of all lady visitors, with whose devotions it must interfere! It has been used within living memory. What would Lady Godiva have said?

The Market Hall at Leominster once occupied a central position in the town, but it was sold to make room for "improvements," and bought by Mr. Arkwright, who re-erected it in its present position and named it "The Grange." The open arcade underneath has been filled in with masonry without concealing the original columns, and the whole has been adapted to the purposes of a modern residence without interference with the design. The principal beam is ornamented with a quaint inscription, half in Latin and half in English, which has been too often reproduced to be repeated here. The fine raised lettering has been picked out with white paint. This is the first building we have come to which is designed and built by John Abell, the carpenter-architect of Hereford, who appears to have been a man of real genius; and it cannot be doubted that he left an indelible mark upon the art and architecture of his county in the seventeenth century. He had probably travelled and seen something of the world, for he was known to King Charles I, and was appointed "one of His Majesty's carpenters," and entrusted with the construction of the defences of Hereford when it stood a siege. No doubt Abell was vastly superior in skill and knowledge

16   OLD COTTAGES, FARM HOUSES, ETC.

to any of his compeers, and that he himself was not altogether unconscious of this superiority may be gathered from the inscription on his tombstone in Sarnesfield churchyard, designed and carved by his own hand, with effigies of himself and his two wives :

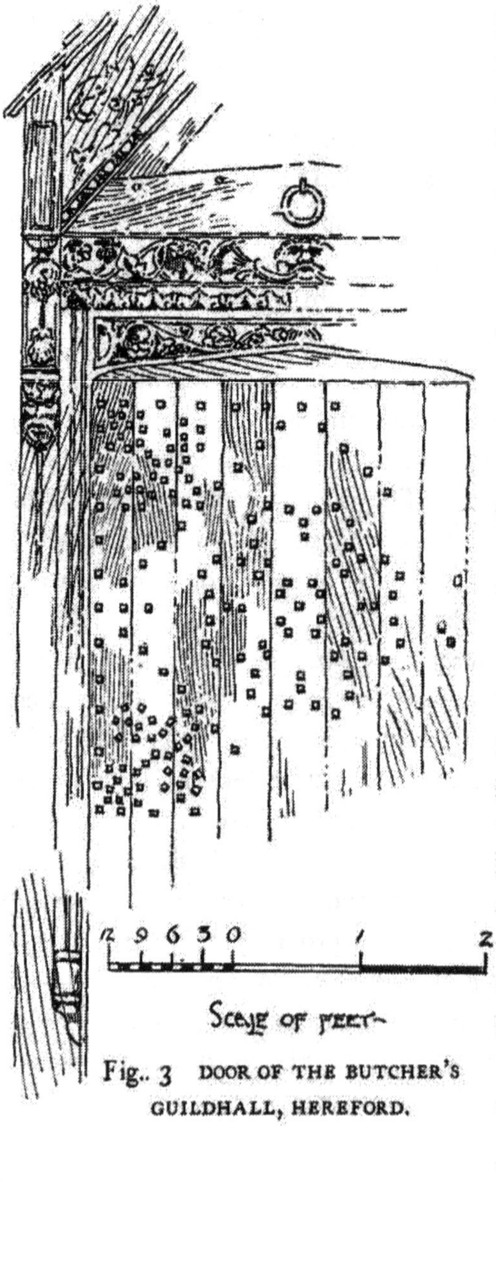

"This craggy stone a covering is for an architect's bed,
That lofty buildings raised high, yet now lies low his head,
His line and rule, so death concludes are locked up in a store,
Build they who list and they who wist, for he can build no more,
His house of clay will hold no longer,
May Heaven's joy build him a stronger."

He was, however, a much better architect than he was a poet, and his work no doubt influenced and elevated the standard of excellence throughout the whole country side, hence a few notes upon his other principal works, although out of order, may not be out of place.

The Hall of the Butcher's Guild at Hereford, Plate

Fig. 3   DOOR OF THE BUTCHER'S GUILDHALL, HEREFORD.

lxix, is dated 1621, and is an ornate and well designed building for the centre of an open space, having three gables at each side and one at each end. The verandah roof carried by posts is entirely modern but otherwise the building is genuine; and the richly carved porch is original and contains a massive oak door, decorated with an effecctive pattern in nail-heads, *see* Figure 3, reminding one of the tattooing of New Zealanders. The upper storey is carried over upon the floor joists at the *sides*, but not at the *ends*, which is the more constructional method. The three tiers of oriels are highly picturesque, with their moulded sills carved out of the solid, as shown in Figure 4. The rope and tassel ornament is repeated upon this and upon several other ancient buildings in the town. Lloyd's Bank now occupies the premises and the richly panelled hall of the Guild still remains.

The Market Hall at Ledbury, Plate lxxii, is a much severer building and stands upon sixteen moulded chestnut columns, Fig. 5, but it does not look quite happy, and seems to be enquiring pathetically what has become of the graceful oriel windows and carved verge boards which John Abell designed for it.

Fig. 4. ORIEL WINDOW AT THE HALL OF THE BUTCHER'S GUILDHALL, HEREFORD.

Another Market Hall of Abell's, and one of rare beauty, stood at the top of the main street at Weobly until forty-five years ago, when it too had to make way for improvements—and no Mr. Arkwright was found to purchase and preserve it. The building which adjoined it is still standing, (Plate lxii), with an air of distinction which confirms the local tradition that it was by the same architect. All that is recorded of it is, that the wife of one Tomkins gave birth here to thirty-three children, all in one room!

A mile or two outside the town of Leominster is Cholstrey, Plate xxxix. A simple country bit, planted on a bank high above the road and shyly retired behind the trees, as if declining the photographer's attentions. The detail shewn in the sketch, Figure 6, is interesting.

On the road towards Pembridge is the ideal village of Eardisland, where we first meet with the river Arrow, spanned by a steep old bridge guarded by a venerable dovecote. The old Rectory, illustrated on Plate xl, is the perfection of timber proportion, and is surrounded by clipped yews which were doubtless planted when the house was young.

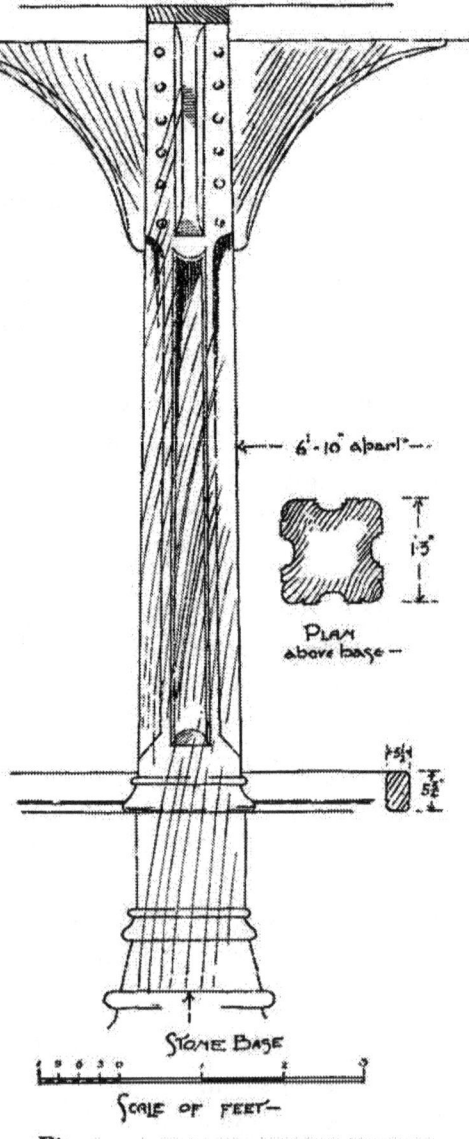

Fig. 5. A COLUMN OF THE MARKET HALL, LEDBURY.

IN HEREFORDSHIRE.

We now enter the village of Pembridge and we may be excused for introducing this somewhat unarchitectural view of the first glimpse of the main street shown on Plate xli. This banking up of the footpath, to get rid of the gradient of the road, and so to form the level base essential to timber architecture, is frequently resorted to.

Plate xlii shews a row of houses near the entrance to the village, while Plate xliii is another view of the same

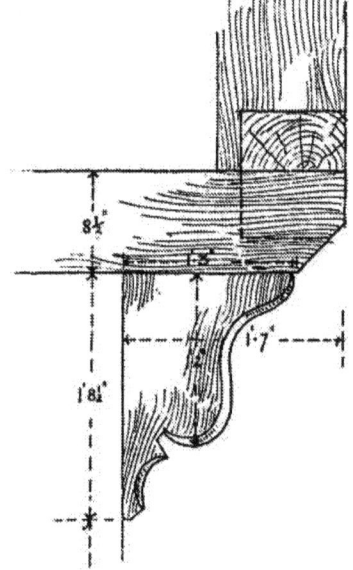

Fig. 6. BRACKET FROM CHOLSTREY.

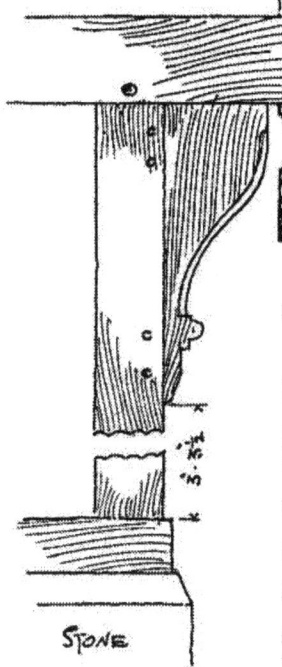

Fig. 7. DETAIL FROM PEMBRIDGE.

group with a second row behind it, which is not cheap and mean, because forced to take a back seat.

The charming roadside house at Pembridge shown on Plates xliv, xlv and xlvi, quite merits the three views devoted to its illustration, as it is a perfect example of the satisfactory effects obtainable with the simplest methods and materials. The absence of carving and moulding, and of shaped timbers is not observed, while the grouping, colouring and light-and-shade are in the highest degree satisfactory. The horizontal weather boards

20 OLD COTTAGES, FARM HOUSES, ETC.

so common in Herefordshire appear here for the first time; Figure 7, shews a bit of detail.

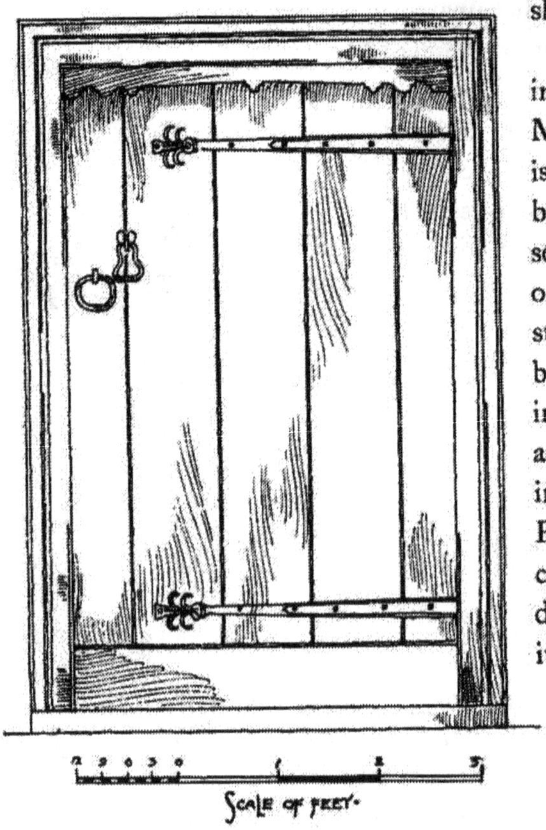

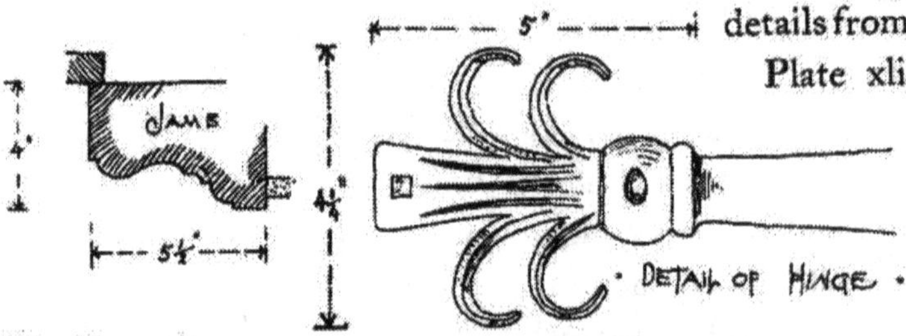

In texture and colouring the Farm House at Middlebrook, Plate xlvii, is the finest group of buildings I have ever seen. The tenant is clamouring for a general restoration, so it should be visited by all who are influenced by poetry in architecture, before the impending destruction. Plate xlviii shews only a common shippon and dovecote combined, but it is more beautiful than any modern building erected during the last hundred years. Figures 8 to 13 give various details from the House. Plate xlix is a row of cottages outside the gates of Middlebrook Farm.

Figs. 8, 9 and 10. DOORWAY AT MIDDLEBROOK, WITH DETAILS.

Cottages at Pembridge (Plate l). This plain, vertical close timbering,

IN HEREFORDSHIRE.

is uncommon in this district, and reminds one forcibly of work to be found in Kent and Sussex. They are well worthy of careful attention, as the effect is perfectly charming, notwithstanding that

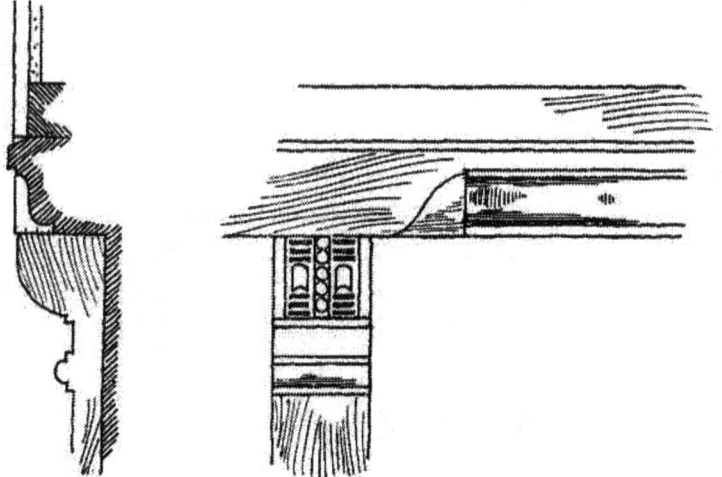

Fig. 11. A BEAM FROM MIDDLEBROOK.

Figs. 12 and 13. BARGEBOARDS FROM MIDDLEBROOK.

the projecting windows have disappeared. Built on a steep decline, these steps to the doorways are required to preserve the continuous horizontal base line.

22 OLD COTTAGES, FARM HOUSES, ETC.

Plate li. These are more delightful cottages at Pembridge. The bold overhanging gable held up its head, no doubt, for several centuries, and these masonry props have been added to support its declining years.

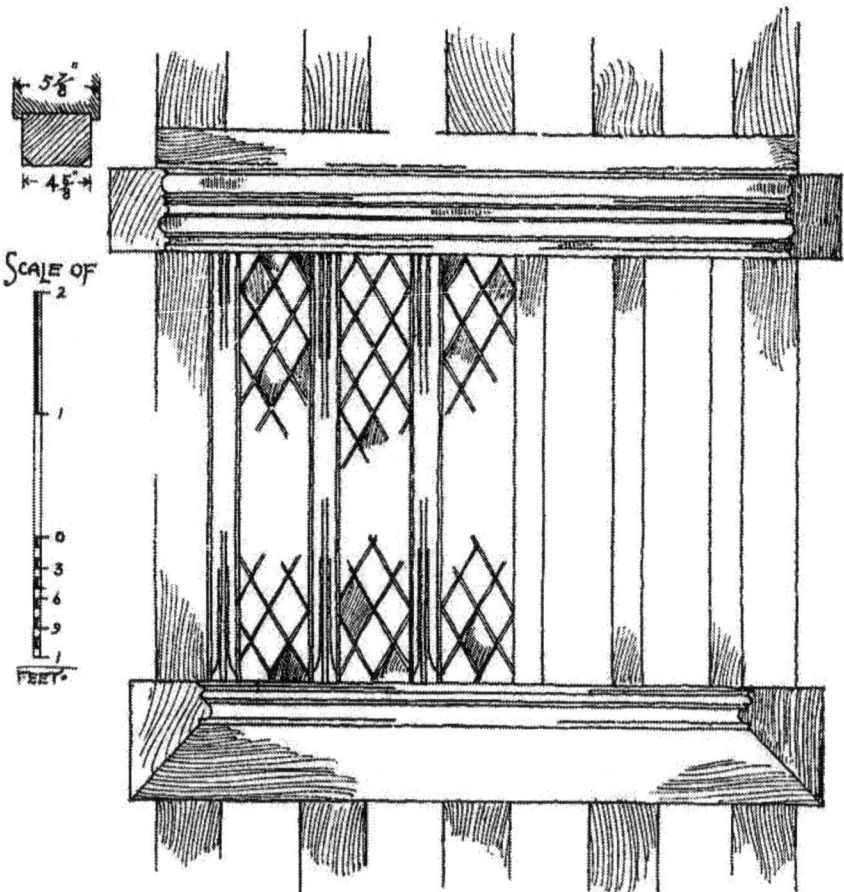

Fig. 14. AN ORIEL WINDOW AT EARDISLEY.

Plate lii is a fine timber Manor House at Luntley, but we dare not give the whole building on account of a huge vulgar, modern bay, which protrudes like a tumour from its fair front. The porch

IN HEREFORDSHIRE.

will give an idea of what the house has been, and it possesses all the Herefordshire characteristics, the weather boarding, the pendants terminating the angle-posts, the massive boldly shaped corbels and the balustrade on three sides.

Plate liii gives the Dovecote adjoining the house at Luntley, a charming and quaint half-timber structure, of a type found with some variations at different places in Herefordshire and Shropshire.

Eardisley is another quaint village, and Plate liv shews a typical row of cottages there. The chimney stacks, which are original, are worthy of attention.

Although the house shewn in Plate lv has been much mutilated, and much of it hidden with roughcast, what remains is untouched and profoundly interesting. The detail is distinctly Gothic in feeling. Figures 14 and 15 illustrate a ground floor Oriel here, which may be seen in the photograph.

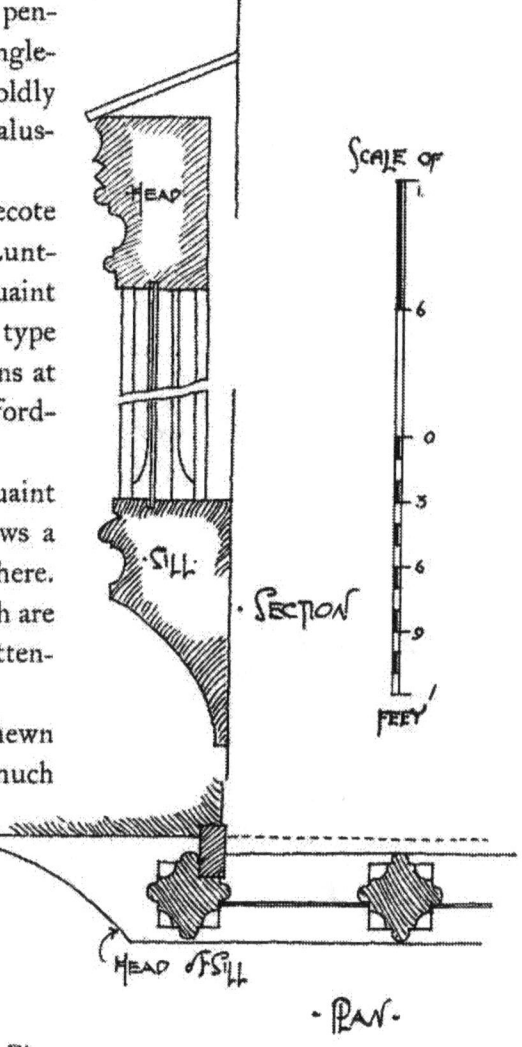

Fig. 15. PLAN AND SECTION OF THE ORIEL SHEWN ON FIG. 14.

We were fortunate in finding the house unoccupied and in obtaining admission, and we found it full of interesting features. Groping about in the dim light of the roofs we discovered an old built-up chapel with the altar step, traceried Gothic holy water stoup, and the original open-timber roof. The barge board from the same village, shewn in the sketch, Figure 16, is equally impressed with Gothic character.

We now reach Weobly, a decaying village, containing quite a collection of fine old timber houses. They are mostly owned by their occupiers, who cannot afford to spend much in keeping them in repair.

Plate lvi is a good example from which to study the value of weather boards. A deeply recessed bay probably occupied the centre of the gable on the ground floor, but this and other interesting features have disappeared.

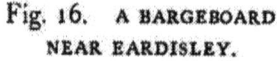

Fig. 16. A BARGEBOARD NEAR EARDISLEY.

Weobly once returned two members to Parliament, and the story goes that previous to the Reform Bill the Marquis of Bath, who owned the whole place, allowed the tenants to live rent free as the price of their votes to his nominee. When Weobly lost its representation, the landlord saw no reason why he should continue to forego his rents and sent his agent to collect them. But a mischievous "opposition" lawyer shewed them that they had become the legal owners of their houses, by having lived in them so long rent free! Now that the houses have fallen into such a sad state of disrepair as to be scarcely habitable, the occupiers have begun for the first time to miss the presence of the landlord and his agent! The Weobly cottages have many local characteristics, and weather boards cast their broad shadows on many a quaint front. To support an overhanging gable by a bracket at one end and by a buttress thrown out from a chimney stack at the other, is a favourite device, (Plate lvii), and the huge timbers forming the gable of this house tell of the days when oak was plentiful.

The Leys Farm, (Plates lviii and lix), is a wonderful specimen of dignified timber architecture, and shews the utmost that can be effected with these materials. It is perfect in texture and colour, most interesting in detail, and no restoration has marred the effect of time upon its silvery beams; while the fact that it has passed into the possession of Sir Joseph Verdin is a guarantee that it will be treated with discrimination and respect. The double tier of pediment-like gables to the bays is almost unique and shews a classic influence, while the Gothic tradition survives in the sills of the gables, which are carried through without any mitreing at the angles. The family of John Brugge, or Bridge, is commemorated in the carved panel over the porch, (Plate lx), together with the date 1589.

Plate lxi, The Rows, Weobly. This is a remarkably interesting group, as it belongs undoubtedly to the fifteenth century. A Gothic traceried window just shews on the side of the far gable, and a drawing in "*The Domestic Architecture of the Middle Ages*," by the author of the "*Glossary of Architecture*," shews that fifty years ago a beautiful traceried three-light window appeared in the gable of the nearest house, and that both the cusped and pierced verge boards remained, while curious cusped panels occupied the ground floor instead of the present doorway and windows. The Gothic doorway in the centre is also proof of the great antiquity of these houses.

Plate lxii, Old House at Weobly. This beautiful example has already been referred to, as one of John Abell's works. The addition of modern shop fronts and poor modern windows cannot render it commonplace, or minimise the effect of its charming proportions and perfect skyline, which from every point of view seem equally faultless.

Plate lxiii. Street Houses, Weobly. This is another very early group, which though much mutilated is full of interest. It has the overhang to front and side and the diagonal angle-beam, which are uncommon in these parts, and also the recessed centre and projecting wings which are common characteristics of the Kent and Sussex houses. The enormous coves are more quaint than beautiful, and the more distant one seems to indicate that the farthest house once formed a third wing, and that the whole block was once under one roof with a uniform line of eaves.

Plate lxiv shews a beautiful and very complete little house, to which the photograph scarcely does justice, owing to the difficulty of obtaining a good point of view, but Plate lxv shews how excellent and thoughtful is the detail of the porch. The manner in which the projecting jambs of the dormer windows terminate with pendants is noteworthy.

The Pigeon House or "Falconry," (as it is locally said to have been), known as "the buttas," is quaint and original, with its ventilating panel of wattle in the gable (Plate lxvi).

Plate lxvii, Wigmore Village. This quaint village is grouped round the hill upon which stands what remains of the Castle of the Mortimers on Offa's Dyke. There are many timber houses, but none possess any distinctive features except the one in the picture, which grows up the hill-side in a delightful natural manner.

Plate lxviii shews a plain well-designed house at Fenhampton, near Weobly, which has probably lost its verge boards and original windows, and seems to protest that it is not dressed to receive visitors!

IN CHESHIRE.

The Hall of the Butcher's Guild and the Market Hall at Ledbury, Plates lxix and lxxii, have already been described (pp. 16 and 17, and Figs. 3, 4 and 5).

The two street houses in Ledbury, Plates lxx and lxxi, throw fine shadows and the one in the narrow Church Lane, Plate lxxi, has interesting details, some of which are given here, Figure 17.

Plate lxxiii is a quaint and entirely genuine example from the neighbourhood of Little Hereford, but it possesses no details which call for remark.

CHESHIRE has always been par excellence the home of timber architecture. Possessed of abundant forests and little good building stone it is not surprising that we find "timber nogging," as they call it there, the style for cottage, mansion and, very often, for the church also. The halls of Adlington, Bramall and Moreton, (Plates xcii, xciii, xciv and c) (with Speke just over the

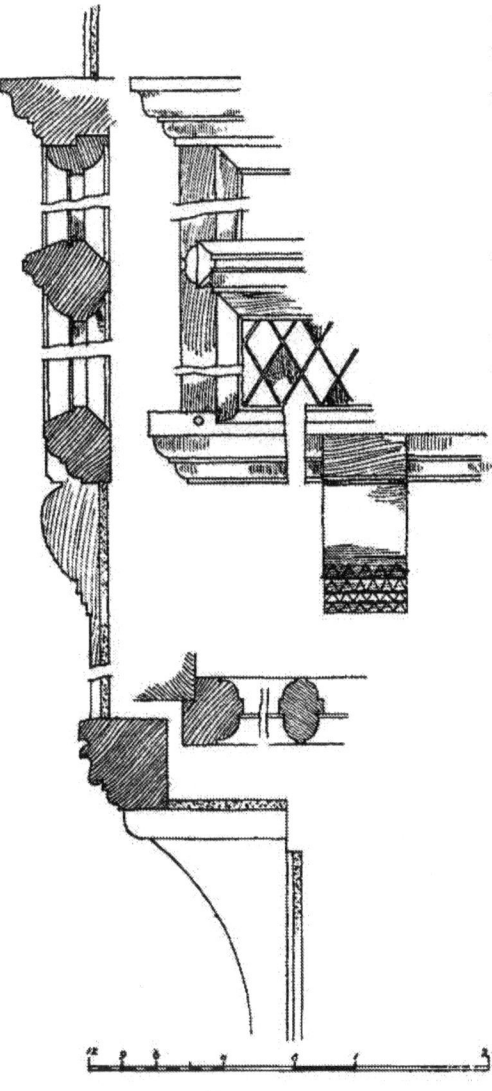

Fig. 17. WINDOWS FROM CHURCH STREET, LEDBURY.

border), are probably the finest timber mansions in the world. These may not all have been of local design, for the carving is often refined and the design original and elaborate, and they are not quite what one would expect from the Cheshire carpenter of those early days; and although "Richard Dale Carpeder" records in carved

Fig. 18. PLASTER GABLE AT WHITEFRIARS—CHESTER.

and painted lettering upon the world-renowned bays of Moreton, that he "made thies windows by the grac of God," he may have had other assistance in designing them! Of the above three mansions we only give some small bits, as they are outside the scope of this modest work, and other fine examples we have had to omit, as being too generally known and frequently illustrated to be of interest. Thus, of picturesque Chester, which was once a veritable black-and-white city, we have only given two examples, which the casual visitor may easily miss: Plate lxxiv, a house in Whitefriars, which is singularly picturesque and retains some interesting plaster work in one of its gables, sketched in Figure 18, and the Stanley Palace, (Plate lxxv), which, having modestly retreated "up an entry," declines to display its complete charms to the widest angled lens! It is a splendid example of the Jacobean Renaissance as applied to timber work, and shews but few traces of the almost forgotten Gothic which dictated its construction.

Duddon Hall, (Plate lxxvi), has a good gable, but unfortunately it has suffered an injudicious restoration since this photograph was taken.

Carden Hall must have been a superb example, and its situation is unrivalled, but it will not now bear a close inspection, although still a great favourite with the amateur. Lower Carden Hall, (Plate lxxvii), a farm-house on the estate, has had the inevitable cleaning up also, but has suffered less permanent injury than its superior. The chimney is quite a work of art, all the crow-steps and gablets being worked with ordinary unmoulded bricks. The herring-bone work in the shafts is a favourite device in these parts.

It is a long jump to Handforth, which is in East Cheshire, (Plate lxxviii). The design of the timbering is not very happy, shewing that even the old architects were not *always* equally successful, but it is undoubtedly genuine and the carved doorway is quite admirable. The sketch, Figure 19, of course gives but a feeble idea of the value and richness of the carving. The house belonged successively to the Handforth and Brereton families and the inscription over the doorway reads thus: "This haulle was buylded in the yeare of oure Lord God mccccclxii by Vryan Breretoun Knight whom maryed Margaret daughter and heyre of Wyllyam Handforth of Handforthe Esquyer and had issue VI sonnes and II dughters."

Alderley Edge is a beautiful spot and it forms quite a centre for the study of timber buildings. "The Eagle and Child," Plate lxxx, just outside the village, has been an inn for centuries, but its license has at last been sacrificed to the conscientious scruples of its noble

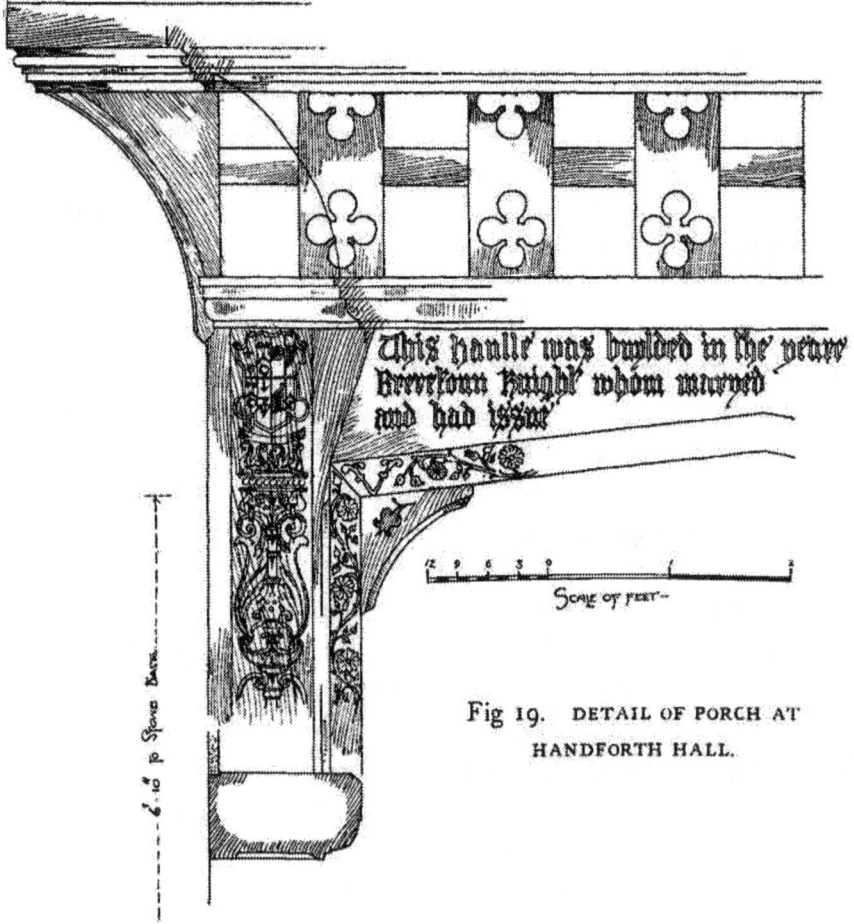

Fig 19. DETAIL OF PORCH AT HANDFORTH HALL.

owner. One cannot help wishing that a less venerable "pub." had been made an example of, and there are plenty to choose from. A portion of the embossed cast lead spout, bearing the date 1688, still

IN CHESHIRE. 31

clings to the eaves, a most interesting and uncommon relic, which is illustrated in Figures 20 and 21.

Plate lxxxi shews one of the numerous Manor Houses of the

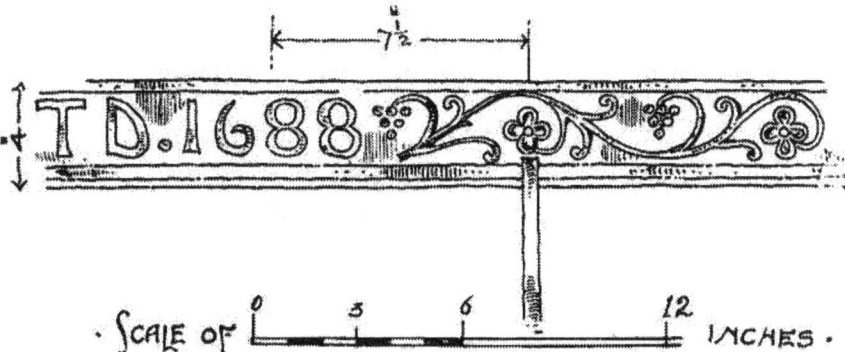

Fig. 20. EMBOSSED LEAD SPOUT FROM THE EAGLE AND CHILD: ALDERLEY EDGE.

Stanley family. Figure 23 gives an effective little bit of ornament and the detail of the window on the left-hand side of the door.

Several delightful cottages adorn the lanes around, (see Plates lxxxi and lxxxii), and the timbering in some of them is unusual and has local fashions, as is so often the case. The draught-board decoration is one of them, (Fig. 22), and it appears again at Swinyard Old Hall, (Plate lxxxv).

The Farm illustrated on Plate lxxxiii is a fine unrestored example, but it is rather gloomy, and the absence of chimneys makes one speculate how the tenants fare when a January blast is whistling through the "wattle-and-dab" of the

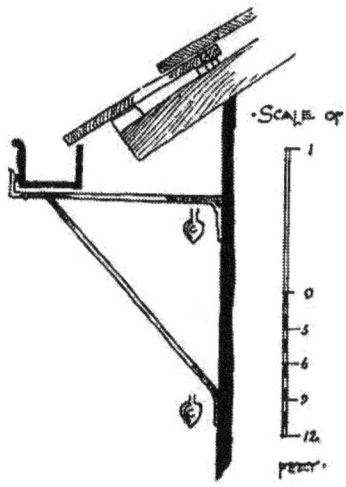

Fig. 21. SECTION OF THE LEAD SPOUT SHOWN ON FIG. 20.

Fig. 22.   A COTTAGE AT ALDERLEY EDGE.

IN CHESHIRE.

walls. Do they appreciate "timber nogging" as much as we do? Woodford Hall, Plate lxxxiv, one of the many homes of the Davenports, is not far away, but it is a great contrast with the last. The beautiful balance of the timbering has a charm which leaves no room for any feeling but admiration. All the house has been modernised with the exception of this fragment. We could not get the fowls in the foreground to understand that they were being photographed! Swinyard lies between Northwich and Warrington. The photograph, Plate lxxxv, was taken on a very dull day and hardly does the old place justice: but it was then or never, as the Restoration *had commenced* and the *scaffold* poles were actually up. The very word suggests a violent end!

Prestbury lies between Macclesfield and Manchester, and this charming little Priest's House, Plate lxxxviii, adorns the main street. It is on a very small scale and has a number of interesting features. The balcony between the two bays is original, though restored. One can picture the priest interviewing his parishioners from hence in his cassock or his nightdress and so saving his legs and the stairs! The four-way gables are very quaint and, so far as I know, unique. Figure 24 shews the plan and the old flagged pavement which survives, and Figure 25 the lead lights.

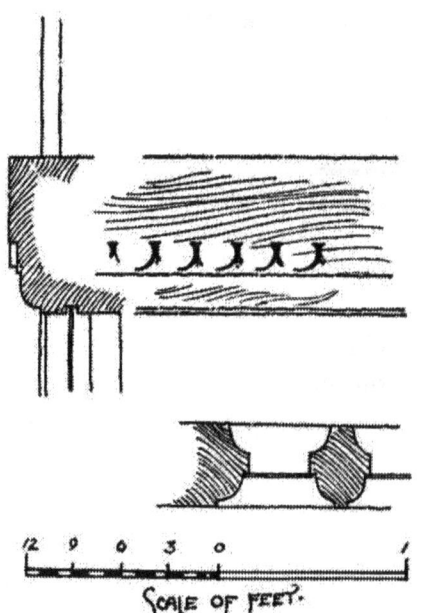

Fig. 23. DETAIL OF BEAM FROM STANLEY HALL.

Driving from Prestbury to Congleton, we come first upon Marton Church, Plate lxxxvii, which is a capital example of timber ecclesiastical architecture. The bloom of age has been roughly brushed aside by the restorer, but he seems to have spared the original timbers and windows. The doorway in the sketch,

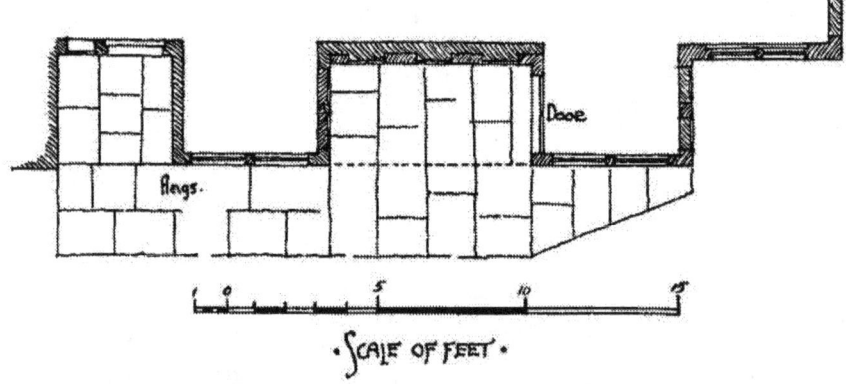

Fig. 24. PLAN OF BAYS AT THE PRIEST'S HOUSE, PRESTBURY.

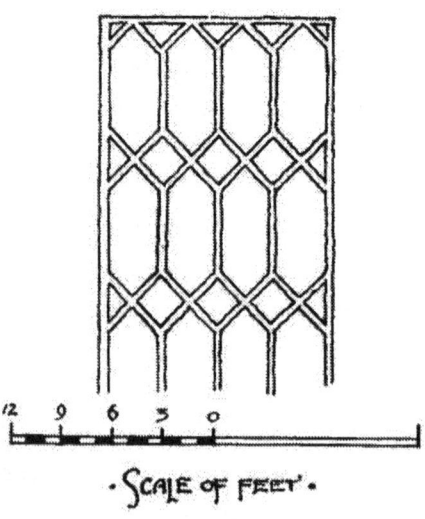

Fig. 25. GLAZING FROM PRESTBURY.

(Figure 26), is interesting, while the hinges are refined and relieve the plainness effectually.

A little further on, among the trees and orchards to the left, we espy Marton Hall, Plate lxxxviii. Charming in design and colour, with roof of sea-weed green, and creamy walls, with the pink blush of brickwork showing through the worn plaster, it formed a picture against the grey-blue sky, never to be forgotten.

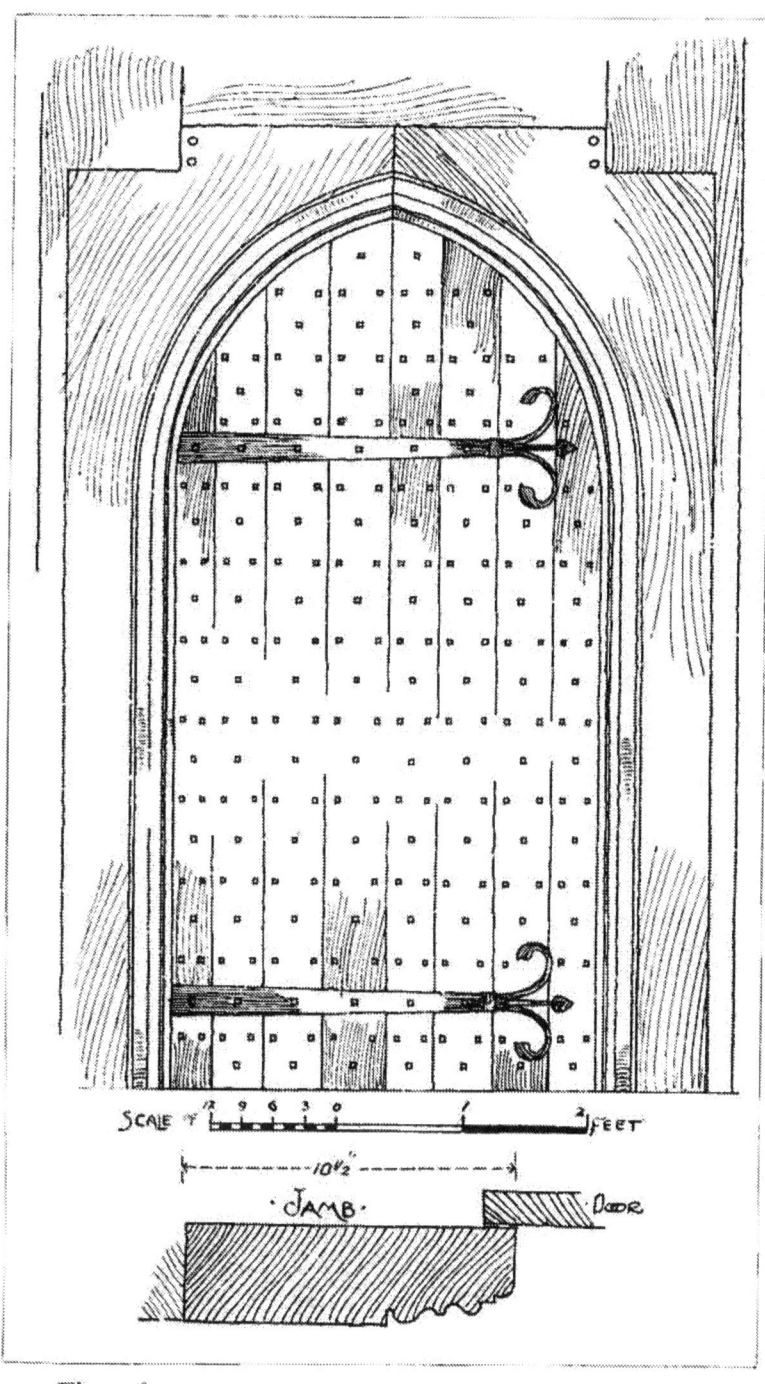

Fig. 26.　DOOR AT MARTON CHURCH, WITH DETAIL.

There is a restraint about the timber work which modern designers would do well to emulate. The inevitable restoration is imminent, and, truth to tell, the rain comes in through the lovely roof and the precious walls, and much of the valuable old furniture has long been kept in oilskin cases! The most exacting member of the Society

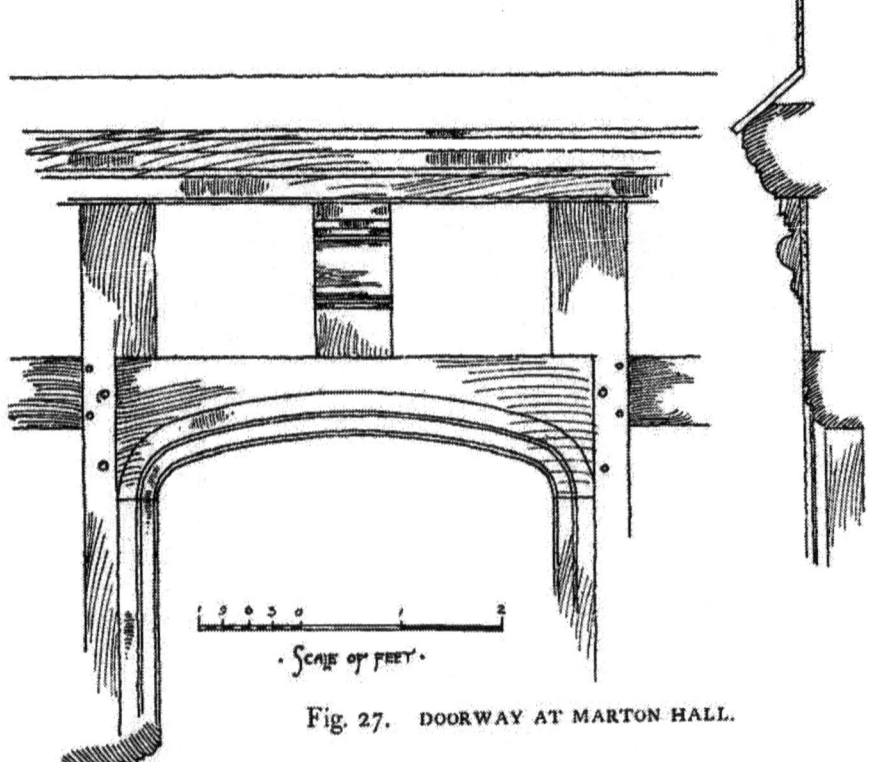

Fig. 27. DOORWAY AT MARTON HALL.

for the Protection of Ancient Buildings would hardly prescribe as the only alternatives—*abandonment* or *oilskins*. The doorway is shewn in Figure 27. Inside there is much that is interesting. The old "dog-gate" remains at the foot of the stairs. We thought that it was there to prevent the children falling down, and wondered that it had not been fixed at the top! A number of Tudor spears still stand in their old rack against the wall. The dining-room is finely panelled, and the fireplace and overmantel are beautiful, and the massive oak table with inlaid sides remains. The back of the house is shewn in Plate xci, and it is as beautiful as the front, although plainer.

Gawsworth is notorious as the place where the church is kept barred and the churchyard secured within circles of unclimbable railing, while visitors to the Rectory are threatened with prosecution for trespass; but the kind lady who lives at the Hall, Plate xc, allows the exterior to be inspected by any one interested in old houses, of which her own is a curious specimen, although scarcely "a thousand years old and all that remains from the fire of 1542," as the gardener told us. The upper projecting chamber is the chapel. The jousting-ground at the back, where for centuries the tournaments were held, remains unchanged.

Plate xci, Weltrough Hall, is one of the many manors of the Davenports. A portion of the moat remains and has been enlarged to form quite a large pond, in which the hall, standing upon an eminence, is charmingly reflected. It has been much mutilated and what remains is only a fragment of the original, but several features (such as a deeply moulded beam) indicate an early origin.

Adlington Hall, Plate xcii, has been the home of the Leghs for generations. The present owner kindly gave us permission to take photographs of the exterior provided we did not ask him to buy them,—a very reasonable condition! He also shewed us the interior, which is charming, especially the Gothic hall, which those familiar with "Nash's Mansions" will remember. Over a gateway is the curious inscription: "A. Do. MCCCCCVRRHVIIXX," the latter half meaning "of the reign of King Henry VII the 20th year," *i.e.* 1505.

Bramall Hall, near Stockport, Plates xciii and xciv, is another splendid old mansion. It belonged originally to the Bromeales or Bromhals, but passed by marriage into the hands of the Davenports in the reign of Edward III. The fine long gallery of which Ormerod gives a sketch taken in 1809 has long disappeared, together with the gatehouse and the fourth side of the quadrangle. The restoration has been, on the whole, judiciously done.

Dutton Hall, Plate xcv, must once have been a splendid place, for it still contains one of the finest banqueting halls in the country, which has been divided up into three storeys of small rooms. The beautiful porch which remains has been so barbarously restored that we have had to go back many years to obtain a photograph fit to produce. Over the doorway is the inscription "Syr Piers Dutton Knyght Lorde of Dutton and my lade dame Julian hys wiff made this hall and buyldyng in ye yere of our Lorde God mcccccxlii who thanketh God of all."

The old Hall at Middlewich, Plates xcvi and xcvii, is a delightful example, and although it has been used for some years as offices to chemical works, it has been tenderly treated and is full of interest.

Sandbach is full of old timber houses, but the restoration mania has been in full swing, and not one dare I present except the old Inn illustrated on Plate xcviii, which, though tampered with and partly sham, has managed to preserve the "grand air."

The old Farm near Alsager, Haslington Hall, Plate xcix, is a fine genuine example in a by-lane, and quite rewarded us for the long hunt we had before it was unearthed.

With the Gatehouse of old Moreton Hall, Plate c, we take leave of our readers, and we feel that we need not apologise for reproducing so familiar an example, for of its matchless proportions and perfect balance it is impossible ever to grow weary.

The question naturally arises, whether timber nogging is a suitable style for a modern house, and as one who has had some experience of such building, I would say that, given a suitable client, one who is worthy of the privilege of living in a timber house, who will appreciate the advantages and put up with the drawbacks—it is an eminently suitable style for a house of moderate dimensions.

But it is not a cheap style, nor one to give to a fidgety or exacting client, who will attribute the natural behaviour of the materials to some neglect on the part of the builder. No matter how dry the oak may be it will shrink and twist to some extent when first exposed to the weather and sunshine. After about two years the oak work will require overhauling and the lead-lights and casements refitting, after which it should give little further trouble, if it has been properly constructed at first. No style of building will harmonize so quickly and so completely with its surroundings and so soon pass through the crude and brand-new period, and none continue to live on such terms of good-fellowship with other materials, whether rosy brickwork, grey lichen-covered masonry, or pearly flag-slates, which last it loves the most of all. And then it is hard to say which season of the year most becomes it. In its cap of virgin snow, in its gorgeous garb of Virginia creeper or in its purple veil of wistaria it is equally bewitching. At the noonday it throws the broadest shadows, and at eve (as no other building can) it gathers on its snowy breast the rose of sunset, and responds to the silver magic of the moon.

FINIS.

SHOPS AT CORNER OF BUTCHERS ROW, SHREWSBURY.

A HOUSE IN BUTCHERS ROW, SHREWSBURY.

A PAIR OF HOUSES IN THE HIGH STREET, SHREWSBURY.

THE COURT HOUSE, SHREWSBURY.

A HOUSE IN MUCH WENLOCK.

Plate V.

HOUSES AND SHOPS IN MUCH WENLOCK.

A CORNER HOUSE IN MUCH WENLOCK.

Plate VII.

THE ABBOT'S HOUSE, MUCH WENLOCK.

BISHOP PERCY'S HOUSE, BRIDGENORTH.

A COTTAGE AT CLEVEDON.

Plate X.

A COTTAGE AT BEWDLEY.

Plate XL.

COTTAGES AT WORFIELD.

Plate XII.

THE GATE-HOUSE, STOKESAY CASTLE.

Plate XIII.

A HOUSE AT CRAVEN ARMS.

Plate XIV.

Plate XV.

END VIEW OF HOUSE AT CRAVEN ARMS.

A DEMOLISHED HOUSE AT CRAVEN ARMS.

Plate XVI.

A GABLE END FROM PITCHFORD HALL.

A HOUSE AT CRESSAGE.

Plate XVIII.

COTTAGES AT BROMFIELD.

Plate XIX.

THE GATE-HOUSE, BROMFIELD PRIORY.

Plate XX.

DODMORE FARM, NEAR LUDLOW.

Plate XXI.

DODMORE FARM, NEAR LUDLOW.

LANE'S HOSPITAL, LUDLOW.

A STREET HOUSE AT LUDLOW.

Plate XXIV.

THE READER'S HOUSE, LUDLOW.

Plate XXVI.

GABLE OF THE BELL INN, LUDFORD.

LUDFORD HOUSE, NEAR LUDLOW.

Plate XXVII.

Plate XXVIII.

A BAY AT LUDFORD HOUSE.

A FARM-HOUSE AT RICHARD'S CASTLE.

Plate XXIX.

ORLETON COURT, HEREFORDSHIRE.

A HOUSE AT ORLETON.

Plate XXXI.

BACK OF "THE SEVEN GABLES," ORLETON.

Plate XXXII.

HOUSE IN THE MAIN STREET, ORLETON.

Plate XXXIII.

COTTAGE IN A LANE AT ORLETON.

Plate XXXIV.

A ROADSIDE HOUSE NEAR ORLETON.

Plate XXXV.

FARM BUILDINGS AT ORLETON.

Plate XXXVI.

THE PORCH AT ORLETON CHURCH.

Plate XXXVII.

"THE GRANGE," LEOMINSTER, FORMERLY THE MARKET HALL.

A FARM HOUSE AT CHOLSTREY.

Plate XXXIX.

THE VILLAGE STREET, PEMBRIDGE.

Plate XLI.

HOUSES AT ENTRANCE TO VILLAGE, PEMBRIDGE.

Plate XLII.

DOUBLE ROW OF COTTAGES, PEMBRIDGE.

Plate XLIII.

FRONT VIEW OF FARM HOUSE, PEMBRIDGE.

Plate XLIV.

END VIEW OF FARM HOUSE, PEMBRIDGE.

Plate XLV.

BACK OF FARM-HOUSE, PEMBRIDGE.

Plate XLVI.

MIDDLEBROOK FARM, NEAR PEMBRIDGE.

Plate XLVII.

FARM BUILDINGS AT MIDDLEBROOK.

Plate XLVIII.

COTTAGES AT MIDDLEBROOK, NEAR PEMBRIDGE.

Plate XLIX.

COTTAGES AT PEMBRIDGE.

COTTAGES AT PEMBRIDGE.

Plate LII.

PART OF FARM-HOUSE, LUNTLEY, NEAR PEMBRIDGE.

Plate LIII.

THE DOVECOTE, LUNTLEY, NEAR PEMBRIDGE.

COTTAGES AT EARDISLEY.

Plate LIV.

A HOUSE AT EARDISLEY.

Plate LV.

A COTTAGE AT WEOBLY.

Plate LVI.

A COTTAGE AT WEOBLY.

Plate LVII.

FRONT VIEW OF "THE LEYS" FARM-HOUSE, NEAR WEOBLY.

SIDE VIEW OF "THE LEYS" FARM-HOUSE.

A DOOR TO "THE LEYS" FARM-HOUSE.

"THE ROWS," WEOBLY.

Plate LXI.

A HOUSE AT WEOBLY.

Plate LXII.

COTTAGES AT WEOBLY.

Plate LXIII.

THE OLD SCHOOL HOUSE, WEOBLY.

Plate LXIV.

PORCH OF THE OLD SCHOOL HOUSE, WEOBLY.

Plate LXVI.

"THE BUTTAS" FALCONRY, NEAR WEOBLY.

IN WIGMORE VILLAGE.

Plate LXVII.

HOUSE AT FENHAMPTON, NEAR WEOBLY.

Plate LXVIII.

THE HALL OF THE BUTCHERS' GUILD, HEREFORD.

CHURCH ROW, LEDBURY.

Plate LXXI.

CLERK'S HOUSES, LEDBURY.

THE MARKET HALL, LEDBURY.

Plate LXXII.

COTTAGES AT LITTLE HEREFORD.

Plate LXXIV.

A HOUSE IN WHITEFRIARS, CHESTER.

Plate LXXV.

THE STANLEY PALACE, CHESTER.

DUDDON HALL, NEAR CHESTER.

LOWER CARDEN HALL, NEAR MALPAS.

Plate LXXVII.

Plate LXXVIII.

HANDFORTH HALL, NEAR CHEADLE.

STANLEY HALL, NEAR CHEADLE.

THE "EAGLE AND CHILD" INN, ALDERLEY EDGE.

Plate LXXX.

Plate LXXXI.

A COTTAGE AT ALDERLEY EDGE.

A COTTAGE AT ALDERLEY EDGE.

Plate LXXXII.

Plate LXXXIII

A FARM-HOUSE AT ALDERLEY EDGE.

Plate LXXXIV.

THE OLD HALL, WOODFORD.

SWINYARD OLD HALL, NEAR KNUTSFORD.

Plate LXXXV.

Plate LXXXVI.

THE PRIETS'S HOUSE, PRESTBURY.

MARTON CHURCH.

FRONT VIEW OF MARTON HALL.

Plate LXXXVIII.

BACK VIEW OF MARTON HALL.

Plate LXXXIX.

GAWSWORTH HALL, NEAR MACCLESFIELD.

WELTROUGH HALL, NEAR MACCLESFIELD.

Plate XCI.

Plate XCII.

ADLINGTON HALL, NEAR MACCLESFIELD.

BRAMHALL HALL, NEAR STOCKPORT.

BRAMHALL HALL, NEAR STOCKPORT.

THE PORCH, DUTTON HALL, NEAR NORTHWICH.

THE OLD HALL, MIDDLEWICH.

Plate XCVI.

Plate XCVII.

A GABLE OF THE OLD HALL, MIDDLEWICH.

THE BOAR INN, SANDBACH.

HASLINGTON HALL, NEAR ALSAGER.

Plate XCIX.

THE GATEHOUSE, MORETON OLD HALL.

Plate C.

www.ingramcontent.com/pod-product-compliance
Lightning Source LLC
Chambersburg PA
CBHW080343170426
43194CB00014B/2665